Kieron Gillen story
Nahuel Lopez art
Nahuel Lopez cover
Digikore Studios color
Kurt Hathaway letters

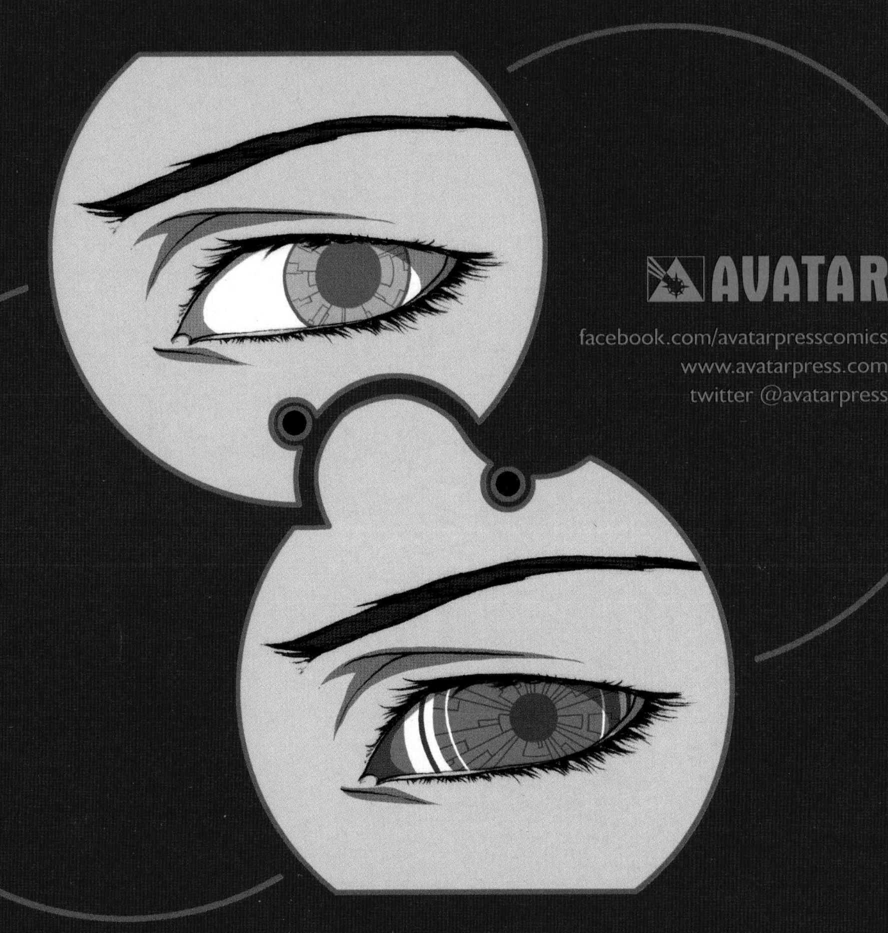

AVATAR
facebook.com/avatarpresscomics
www.avatarpress.com
twitter @avatarpress

William Christensen editor-in-chief
Ma
Ari

chapter 7

S: STATUS UPDATE
MED ROBBERY.
TAG: TARGET UPDATE
ALL TARGETS SHOW MINOR REFLEX UPGRADES AND HEAVY BLACK CRYSTAL SIGNATURES. COMBAT DATA WILL BE SEQUESTERED FOR ONGOING INVESTIGATION INTO INCREASE IN BLACK CRYSTAL CONTRABAND. CREDIT WILL BE ADDED TO YOUR ACCOUNT AFTER THE ARREST.
TAG: TARGET 1
TAG: TARGET 2
AG: TARGET 3
TAG: TACTICAL ADVICE
AMBUSH WITH FATAL FORCE. 95% PROBABILITY OF SUCCESS.
I'M POLICE.
YES, YOU WOULD THINK THAT. YOU'RE RETIRED MILITARY CRYSTAL. THAT'S HOW YOU WORK.

DROP THE WEAPONS AND DEACTIVATE YOUR FUCKING CRYSTAL! FUCKING *NOW!*
YOU HAVE THREE SECONDS TO NOT DIE!

STATUS UPDATE
BABILITY OF
CESS: 75%.
TAG: STATUS UPDATE
PROBABILITY OF SUCCESS: 25%.
HEY, LUIZA. HAVE YOU EVER THOUGHT ABOUT TRYING AB-3? THE ASPIRATIONAL DRINK FOR YOUNG EXTRATERRESTRIAL PROFESSIONALS!

FUCK!
TAG: PERSONAL LOG
NOT SURE BUYING AD-SUPPORTED CRYSTAL IN MY LINE OF WORK WAS THE BEST IDEA.
GET OFF! LET ME FINISH HER!
FUCK OFF! WE *PAID* FOR THIS. I WANT TO SEE WHAT IT CAN DO.
TAG: PERSONAL LOG
BUT I COULDN'T AFFORD THE LATEST VISUAL PROCESSING APPS, AND MY MILITARY-GRADE SUITE DOESN'T EXACTLY DO THE PRETTIES.
FUCKING *DISMISS!*
TAG: PERSONAL LOG
STILL... A LITTLE FREE READ/WRITE SPACE FOR MICROAPPS...
WHO YOU DISMISSIN'?
TAG: DIALOGUE PLUGIN OPTION!
1] IRONIC.
2] SERIOUS.
3] STOIC.

NOW?
TAG: STATUS UPDATE
SYNTHETIC MYOFIBER OUTPUT: 258%.
NOBODY.
TAG: STATUS UPDATE
PROBABILITY OF SUCCESS: 65%.
TAG: PERSONAL LOG
FOR EXAMPLE, THE FREE RETRO ACTION-MOVIE DIALOGUE MICROAPP. DIDN'T WANT TO PAY FOR ANY UPGRADES, THOUGH I'LL ADMIT BEING ABLE TO SAY APPROPRIATE SHAKESPEAREAN ZINGERS AT WORK WOULD HAVE ITS APPEAL.

DROP THE FUCKING KNIFE.
TAG: STATUS UPDATE
SYNTHETIC MYOFIBER OUTPUT: 146%.
TAG: STATUS UPDATE
PROBABILITY OF SUCCESS: 95%.
NINETY-FIVE PERCENT?
WHY NOT ONE HUNDRED?

OH YEAH.
A FOURTH TARGET.
TAG: STATUS UPDATE
PROBABILITY OF SUCCESS: 100%.
CONGRATULATIONS, LUIZA.
YOUR ACCOUNT HAS BEEN CREDITED WITH TWO ARRESTS AND TWO FORCIBLE CEASING OF HOSTILITIES.
THEY'VE GOT MUCH BETTER SKILL CRYSTALS THAN PLUG CRIMINALS SHOULD.
ARE WE ANY CLOSER TO FINDING OUT WHERE ALL THE BLACK CRYSTAL IS COMING FROM?

OTHER FREELANCERS ARE WORKING ON IT, LUIZA. I'M SURE THEY'RE MAKING INCREDIBLE PROGRESS.
AM *I* ANY CLOSER TO WORKING ON THAT, GRAPEVINE?
I'M SORRY, LUIZA. YOUR PERSONALITY SKILL-SET IS MUCH MORE SUITED FOR YOUR PRESENT WORK.
ANYTHING ELSE AVAILABLE?
YES, LUIZA! THERE'S A MISSION AVAILABLE IN YOUR VICINITY!
POLICE-RELATED WORK.
OF COURSE, LUIZA. YOUR CHOICE IN MISSION PARAMETERS ARE ALREADY IN YOUR PREFERENCES. I DON'T MAKE SILLY MISTAKES LIKE THAT.
OKAY. WHAT HAVE YOU GOT?
ASSISTING IN THE TRANSPORTATION OF TWO BODIES TO THE MORGUE.

TAG: HOTSIDE CENTRAL 57
MOBILE HQ OF HOTSIDE HEAT, FOLLOWING BELT WORKER MIGRATION.
HEY, LUIZA.
USER NOTES: SIMON HARKING
TOPSIDE MILITARY LIAISON. MEMORIES DELETED. INCREDIBLY BAD NEWS. IF YOU EVER SPEAK TO HIM AGAIN, YOU WILL REGRET IT IN A LIFE-CHANGING WAY. ALSO: TINY PENIS. TINY, TINY PENIS.
WHAT'S UP?
HI.
DID THEY HAVE BLACK CRYSTAL?
N'GAI ROBINS BROUGHT ME DOWN TO DRILL ME ABOUT IT, THINKING IT MAY BE A MILITARY LEAK, BUT THERE ARE NO SIGNATURES. IT'S ENTIRELY FLAWLESS BLACK...
RIGHT.
WAIT... LUIZA. YOU BLANKING ME?
WAIT-- HAVE YOU *BLANKED* ME?

YES. I AM, AND, YES I HAVE.
I HEARD SOME BAD THINGS ABOUT YOU.
FROM A TRUSTWORTHY PERSON?
STATUS UPDATE: BLANKED
COLLOQUIAL SLANG FOR THE DELETION OF CRYSTAL-STORED MEMORIES ATTACHED TO AN EX.
THEY'VE GOT A HISTORY OF BAD JUDGEMENT, BUT FOR ONCE I'M BELIEVING THEM.
HEY-- N'GAI!
STATUS UPDATE: NUCLOSE RECHARGE
FOR ARTIFICIAL MYOFIBER-EQUIPPED AGENTS, A SUFFICIENT ENHANCED QUASI-GLUCOSE SUBSTRATE ("NUCLOSE") RESERVOIR IS REQUIRED.
WELL, IF IT ISN'T THE SAVIOUR OF THE PLANET.
GOOD ARREST, I HEAR.
THANKS. BUT... I HEARD YOU TALKED TO HARKING ABOUT THE CRYSTAL.
IF IT'S FLAWLESS BLACK, IT'S COMING DIRECTLY FROM A MANUFACTURER.

YOU'RE RIGHT. WE'RE ON THE CASE. IF IT'S OFF-PLANET, WE'RE SOURCING ROUTES. IF IT'S ON-PLANET... WELL, WE'RE JUST GOING TO HAVE TO BE METHODICAL AND HIT UP EACH POSSIBLE SITE, PLUS TRY AND FIND THE ILLEGAL ONES.
IF IT'S AN ILLEGAL ONE, I WORRY. THERE IS A *LOT* OF CRYSTAL THERE, SOLD DIRT CHEAP. I WOULDN'T THINK MANY CRIMINALS COULD AFFORD A CRYSTAL PLANT THAT BIG.
HOW ABOUT, THE MERCUROISA--
LUIZA. *I KNOW.* THIS IS ALL I'VE DEALT WITH FOR THE LAST MONTH.
I KNOW YOU WANT TO HELP, BUT *I KNOW.*
I'LL DO MY WORK. YOU DO YOUR WORK. AND YOU ARE MAKING AN IMPACT. YOU'RE HITTING THE NUMBERS HARD.
I'M MAINLY JUST *HITTING*.
I WANT TO HELP. I MEAN, WITH MY PERSONALITY CLASSIFICATION IT'S ALWAYS GOING TO BE UPHILL, BUT MAYBE I COULD DO SOME VOLUNTEER WORK, PRO BONO.
I LIKE YOU, LUIZA. EVEN PEOPLE WHO DON'T LIKE YOU RESPECT YOU. YOU SAVED THE PLANET.
BUT IF YOU TURN SCAB, FUCK YOU.
LUIZA BORA! MISSION ALERT!
WE HAVE AN ASSIGNMENT THAT FITS YOUR SKILL-SET PERFECTLY!

I'M NOT GOING TO CLEAN LATRINEBOTS.
NO, LUIZA! THIS IS A CLASS A+ CASE, WITH A HIGH BASAL WAGE WITH VARIOUS POSSIBLE UPGRADES IF THE MISSION DEVELOPS.
THE DIO-42 WEAPON RESEARCH BASE HAS LOST CONTACT. WE'D LIKE YOU TO INVESTIGATE.
DIO-42 WOULD INCLUDE MILITARY GRADE HARDWARE...
COULD THIS BE TO DO WITH THE CRYSTALS?
POSSIBLY, LUIZA. YOUR INTEREST IN *THAT* CASE HAS CERTAINLY IMPACTED YOUR SELECTION FOR THIS ONE.
THERE'S A 7% CHANCE THAT THIS IS RELEVANT TO THAT INVESTIGATION. THERE IS A 32% CHANCE IT IS A CRITICAL EVENT REQUIRING EXTREME SKILLS LIKE YOURS TO SURVIVE.
THERE IS A 58% CHANCE THAT A LOSS OF TECH FAILURE IS RESPONSIBLE FOR THEIR DROPPING OUT OF CONTACT (AND A 50% CHANCE OF THAT BEING FIXED BY THE TIME YOU ARRIVE THERE). THERE IS A 10% CHANCE EVERYONE WILL ALREADY BE DEAD DUE TO CATASTROPHIC TECHNICAL FAILURE. THERE IS--
OKAY. DO I GET A PARTNER?
WE HAVE NO ACCESS TO QUALIFIED COMBAT TECHNICIANS WITHIN THIS MISSION'S BUDGET. AS SUCH, WE'LL BE PROVIDING A SOUL COPY OF A QUALIFIED TECH TO PROVIDE THE REQUISITE SKILLS.
OH, GREAT....
SOULS ARE *CREEPY*.

AND... DONE.
OKAY: TECHNICIAN CRYSTAL ACTIVATE.
HEY, LUIZA! LONG TIME!
LUCAS.
I SOLD MY PERSONALITY IMPRINT. SOUL COPYRIGHTS ARE EXPENSIVE.
PAID FOR THE BAR TAB, Y'KNOW?
GRAPEVINE!

YES, LUIZA?
NO!
LUIZA-- WHILE WE SEE THAT THE SOUL-IMPRINT SIMULATION OF LUCAS ANSOM CAUSES YOU CONSIDERABLE AGITATION, YOUR LAST PAIRING WAS ENORMOUSLY SUCCESSFUL!
HE BETRAYED US! HE WAS FEEDING INFORMATION TO THE MERCURIOSA!
HE'S SEXIST IN AN EARLY TWENTY-FIRST-CENTURY MANNER!
HOWEVER, YOU SAVED THE WORLD TOGETHER.
WITH OUR LIMITED DATA SET OF YOU SAVING THE WORLD, WE CAN'T POSSIBLY KNOW WHAT WAS THE CRITICAL ELEMENT. AS SUCH, REMOVING ANYTHING FROM THE WINNING COMBINATION AT THIS POINT WOULD BE PREMATURE.
C'MON. I'M EVEN BETTER THAN THE REAL THING.
PLUS: I CAN'T EVEN LEER AT YOU ANYMORE. BONUS!
THIS IS JUST NOT ACCE--
LUIZA. UNDERSTAND, LUCAS IS SOMEWHAT *INEXPENSIVE* IN CRYSTAL TECH TERMS. BY USING HIM, THE RESOURCES SAVED CAN BE REASSIGNED TO YOUR FEE.
WITHOUT THAT SAVING, YOU WOULDN'T BE ON THIS TASK.
OKAY.
LET'S GET THIS OVER WITH.

TAG: HOTSIDE
TEMPERATURE = VERY.
TAG: THE DIO-42 BASE
532 RESEARCH SCIENTISTS IN EXPERIMENTAL CRYSTAL AND BIOENHANCEMENT.
OUT OF CONTACT FOR 23 HOURS.

HEY! GIMME SOME OPTICS HERE!
TAG: STATUS UPDATE
LIGHT INTENSIFIER ACTIVATED. SORRY, LUIZA.
A CRASHED SHIP. THAT'S A BAD OMEN, ISN'T IT?
SOMEONE WAS TRYING TO GET AWAY IN A *HURRY*.

RECORDING CHIP. SEEMS WE GOT OURSELVES A CLUE.
I DON'T KNOW WHAT WE'D DO WITHOUT YOUR UNDEAD TECHNICAL EXPERTISE, LUCAS.
OKAY. PULSE THE REPORT UP GRAPEVINE VIA THE SHIP, AND PLAY IT.
AND OPEN THE DOOR.
YOU GODDIT.
I'M TONY ARUBA.
I'M NOT SURE WHAT'S GONE WRONG.

I WAS OUTSIDE THE BASE DOING MINOR REPAIRS WHEN WHATEVER HAPPENED HAPPENED. ALL I HEARD WAS SCREAMING OVER THE COMMS ABOUT HALF THE STAFF GOING CRAZY AND ATTACKING PEOPLE...
THEN SILENCE.
I STAYED OUT HERE UNTIL I WAS NEARLY OUT OF OXYGEN, HOPING I'D GET A MESSAGE, BUT NOTHING.
I'M GOING TO GO AND SEE WHAT' HAPPENING. IF IT STILL BAD I'M GOING TO TRY A GET TO THE MA COMMS ROOM A SEND AN UPDAT TO THE GRAPEVINE.
IF SOMETHING'S WRONG WITH THE SPIRE AND I CAN'T, I'LL TRY TO HIDE THERE AND HOPE SOMEONE IS ACTIVE IN SECURITY.
OKAY, LUCAS...
GIVE ME A ROUTE TO COMMS CENTRAL.

AFFIRMATIVE!
JUST LOOK AT THIS PLACE! IS THIS CAMERON OR ROMERO? I'M GETTING DISTINCT VIBES HERE.
I'M BETTING ROMERO.
I'M NOT SURE WHETHER I PREFER YOU WHEN YOU'RE DEAD OR ALIVE.
PRO-- NO SEX DRIVE. ANTI-- NO INHIBITIONS.
EITHER WAY YOU'RE FUCKED.
SHUSH. PLEASE, SHUSH.
ONLY YOU CAN HEAR ME, DON'T WORRY, I--
OH, FUCK.
OH, WOW!

OKAY, I WAS OFF.
NOT ROMERO.

FFFFFFUUUUCCCCKKKKK!

ENNIS/BURROWS.

MERCURY HEAT:

ANOTHER BLOODY CROSSOVER

chapter 8

S: STATUS UPDATE
ZA BORA, INVESTIGATING LOSS CONTACT WITH RESEARCH BASE. COVERS WHAT APPEARS TO BE T CENTURY CLASSIC HORROR NSTERS "THE CROSSED".
DROP THE FUCKING WEAPONS! NOW!
CUNTTTZZZ
KILL CUNTZZZ COPS
KNIFE-FUCK! FUCK! FUCK!
FUCK CUNTS, LUIZA! THEY'RE CROSSED!
THEY'RE NOT GOING TO ROP THE SEVERED MB AND STEP AWAY ROM THE VIOLATED CORPSE!
THERE'S NO SUCH THING AS CROSSED.
I'M POLICE. THEY GET A WARNING.
WHAT THE

TAG: STATUS UPDATE
COMBAT MODS ACTIVE. INCOMING TARGETS. SOMATIC RESPONSE ENHANCERS ACTIVATED.
WHAT AM I DOING?

I'M MAKING ARRESTS.
ARE YOU CRAZY?
THEY'VE TURNED CROSSED! ALL BETS ARE OFF!
OR... IS THIS SMART? DON'T WANT TO ALERT THE REST?
GOOD THINKING!

DON'T LET THEM GET ANY SALIVA ON YOU!
OR SPUNK!
BE CAREFUL WITH THE SPUNK!
I'M A 37-YEAR-OLD WOMAN.
YOU DON'T NEED TO WARN ME ABOUT THE DANGERS OF SEMEN.
TAG: STATUS UPDATE
SYNTHETIC MYOFIBER OUTPUT: 176%.
I KNOW HOW TO USE PROTECTION.
TAG: STATUS UPDATE
TARGETS DISABLED COMBAT MODS DEACTIVATED.

Y ARE YOU MAKING JOKES AND T FILLING YOUR PANTIES WITH THE EST COMBAT-ENHANCED SHIT? 'RE TRAPPED IN A BASE ALONE WITH A BUNCH OF CROSSED!
YOU ARE LITERALLY AND FIGURATIVELY FUCKED!
THEY'RE NOT CROSSED.
THE CROSSED ARE JUST STORIES.
THEY'RE PEOPLE WITH CROSSES ON THEIR FACES WHO WERE IN THE PROCESS OF FUCKING A CORPSE.
THEY'RE FUCKING CROSSED!
REALITY AND FANTASY.
KNOW THE FUCKING DIFFERENCE.
AND THE DAY I CAN'T TAKE DOWN THREE HUMAN-NORMAL OUT-OF-SHAPE SCIENTISTS IS THE DAY I'D BE FINE WITH BEING EATEN.
NOW... LET'S SEE...
EYES UP, LUIZA!

A ROOM FULL OF FANTASY, COMING RIGHT AT YOU!

THAT ONE HAS-- OOOH-- SIX AND A HALF INCHES OF ENGORGED FANTASY.
TAG: STATUS UPDATE
FLIGHT MODE ACTIVATED.
THAT FANTASY IS WEARING SOMEONE ELSE'S FANTASTICAL FACE NAILED ON!
SHUT UP!
I'M GIVING FANTASTICAL TACTICAL ADVICE.
I MEAN, IT'D BE TERRIBLE IF THERE WAS A FANTASY BLOCKADE OF MURDEROUS RAPISTS ON THE WAY TO THE AIRLOCK...
I IMAGINE IN THE LAST FEW SECONDS YOU'D SAY "I WISH THAT I LISTENED TO LUCAS WARNING ME ABOUT THE CROSSED. HE WAS DEFINITELY ONTO SOMETHING!"
LUCKY FOR YOU, NOT A CROSSED IN SIGHT!
WHEN I GET YOU EXTRACTED, I'M GOING TO CRUSH YOU WITH A HAMMER.

TOUCHY!
SEAL THE FUCKING DOOR.
CROSSED CAN OPEN DOORS. THEY RE HIGHER SKILLS.
LET'S HOPE THEIR SKILLS ARE LOWER THAN YOURS.
OH YEAH. I'M A HACK HACKER AND THEY'RE A BASE FULL OF SCIENTISTS.
I'M SURE I'M BETTER THAN ALL OF THEM--
AND WE DON'T KNOW THEY'RE CROSSED!
CROSSED IS THE SORT OF STUFF MY BROTHER OBSESSED OVER.
I HATED THOSE MOVIES!
IT WAS ACTUALLY A COMIC ORIGINALLY.
OF COURSE IT WAS.
LUIZA... BAD NEWS. LOOK OUTSIDE.

YOU SEE, THE CROSSED KEEP ALL THE SKILLS OF THEIR PREVIOUS LIFE, BUT WITHOUT ANY INHIBITIONS. SEEING THE TRANSPORT ARRIVE, ONE OF THEM MUST HAVE THOUGHT IT WAS FINE FOR A JOYRIDE--
FUCKING FUCKING SHUT THE FUCK UP.

SYSTEM--
INCREASE THE EMOTIONAL BLINKERS ON NEGATIVE EMOTIONS.
TAG: STATUS UPDATE
EXTREMES OF DEPRESSION, FEAR, ANXIETY TETHERED. WE WILL KEEP YOU UP TO DATE ON YOUR FLUCTUATIONS OF STRESS VIA YOUR HUD.
SO... YOU GOING TO OPEN THE DOOR AND GO DOWN SHOOTING?
NO.
YOU'RE GOING TO KEEP THE DOOR SHUT AND *I'M* GOING TO WAIT.
I'M MISSING. THERE'LL BE A RESCUE MISSION SOON.
AND WHEN I FAIL TO KEEP THE DOOR CLOSED...?

I DON'T AVE ENOUGH BULLETS.
I'LL KILL A BUNCH AND THEN THEY'LL KILL ME. EITHER WAY I'M DEAD, AND I'VE KILLED INNOCENT CIVILIANS FOR NO REASON.
OKAY-- LET'S SAY THEY'RE NOT CROSSED. WHAT IF THEY'RE JUST PEOPLE ON DRUGS ACTING FUCKED UP? OR A KIND OF FANCY DRESS PARTY THAT'S GONE LORD OF THE FLIES?
WHAT IF THEY ***ARE*** JUST A BUNCH OF CRIMINALS?
WE DON'T KNOW.
POLICE. EVIDENCE.
WOW. ARE YOU SOME KIND OF HERO?

SERIOUSLY, YOU'RE GOING TO LET THEM TEAR YOU APART? THAT'S ABOVE AND BEYOND.
WHO ARE YOU?
I'M VIKA COX.
I MANAGED TO SEAL MYSELF THE SECURITY HQ WHEN IT ALL START. BEEN HOLED UP EVER SINCE.
WHAT HAPPENED?
IS IT SOME KIND OF BIOPLAGUE OR...
I DON'T KNOW. THEY WORK ON A LOT OF SKEEVY STUFF HERE. COULD BE ANY NUMBER OF THINGS.
I'M JUST A CRYSTAL TECHNICIAN. I DON'T KNOW ANYTHING...
TAG: STATUS UPDATE
HOLOCOMMS LINK ACCEPTED.
WHY DIDN'T YOU CALL FOR HELP?
COMMS ARE DOWN. DON'T KNOW WHY. MOST OF THE SYSTEMS SEEM TO BE FINE, BUT THERE'S SOMETHING BETWEEN WHERE I AM AND THE CORE COMMUNICATION SPIRE THAT'S GONE HAYWIRE.
IF YOU COULD GET TO IT, YOU'D BE ABLE TO ACCESS THE TRANSMITTER DIRECTLY...
THAT WOULD INVOLVE GETTING PAST ALL OF THE INFECTED.
THEY'RE CALLED "CROSSED", LUIZA.

I... I COULD OPEN MY DOOR, GO OUT, AND MAKE SOME NOISE. THEY'LL COME RUNNING TO ME.
IT COULD THIN THE HERD ENOUGH SO YOU CAN MAKE A RUN FOR IT...
I CAN'T THINK OF A BETTER OPTION. THANK YOU, VIKA.
LUCAS-- GIVE ME THE ROUTE.
OKAY... GET READY. AND I WARN YOU, YOU'RE GOING TO SEE SOME REALLY HORRIBLE STUFF OUT THERE...
NO. I'M NOT.

RUN THE IMAGE PROCESSING CENSOR.
I DON'T WANT TO SEE...
ANY RAPE. ANY RESULTS OF RAPE. ANY VIOLATED CORPSES. ANY CORPSES IN THE PROCESS OF BEING VIOLATED. ANY GENITALIA WHATSOEVER.
HORSECOCK! DON'T FORGET TO MENTION HORSECOCK.
ONE-- WHERE ARE THEY GOING TO GET A HORSE FROM, LUCAS?
TWO-- ALREADY INCLUDED IN THE LARGER CATEGORY OF GENITALIA.
DEPLOY FILTER.
OKAY-- I'M GOING OUT THERE. GOOD LUCK!
YOU TOO. WHEN WE GET THROUGH THIS, THE AB-1 IS ON ME.
TAG: STATUS UPDATE
CENSOR ACTIVE AS PER USER-DEFINED SETTINGS.

LUCAS--
GIVE ME A
PEEK.
WELL COCK ME WITH
A FUCKHAMMER. IT'S
WORKING.
LUCAS--
OPEN THE
DOOR.

I'VE SEALED MYSELF IN AGAIN. I'M FINE. THEY'LL BE COMING BACK TO YOU.
ARE YOU OKAY?
I'M FINE.

TAG: THE SPIRE
MAIN COMMUNICATOR AND LOCALISED AI-PROCESSING CORE. ESSENTIAL FOR MAINTAINING CRYSTAL MANUFACTURE.

HOW'RE YOU GOING TO GET UP THERE?
OH YEAH.
TAG: STATUS UPDATE
SYNTHETIC MYOFIBER OUTPUT: 210%.
THAT.
TAG: STATUS UPDATE
POST-HUMAN PARKOUR ENGAGED.
TAG: STATUS UPDATE
BOING—BOING—BOING.
AM I GOING TO HAVE TO RESET YOU?

TAG: STATUS UPDATE
ER... NO. PARKOUR OFF.
GRAPEVINE! THIS IS LUIZA BORA!
REPORTING A LEVEL 4 COLLAPSE OF CIVILIZATION IN THE FACILITY. NEED HELP, IMMEDIATELY!

ER...

IT'S DEAD.
LUIZA TO VIKA.
IT'S NOT WORKING...
OH GOD. THAT'S... YOU'RE TRAPPED THERE.
I'M SORRY. I'LL SEE WHAT WE CAN WORK OUT.

GOOD LUCK.

OH, GOD...
TAG: STATUS UPDATE
THIS IS YOUR REQUESTED PHYSIOLOGICAL STRESS WARNING.

...THIS IS SO FUCKING COOL.
CROSSED

chapter 9

NAHUEL LÓPEZ

THE DIO-42 BASE
RESEARCH SCIENTISTS IN
PERIMENTAL CRYSTAL AND
ENHANCEMENT.
OF CONTACT FOR 23 HOURS.
ZA BORA, INVESTIGATING,
COVERS APPARENT REAL-LIFE
ECTION OF 21ST CENTURY HORROR
ARACTERS "THE CROSSED."
IT'S BEEN GREAT WORKING WITH YOU, LUIZA.

MAYBE WE'LL GET TOGETHER ANOTHER TIME?
I MEAN, IF YOU'VE SOLD YOUR PERSONALITY FOR A SOUL PRINT WE COULD BE DOING THIS TOGETHER... *FOREVER!*
WOULDN'T THAT BE AMAZING?
MAMA WAS RIGHT.
IT COULD ALWAYS BE WORSE.
FUCK THIS.
TAG: STATUS UPDATE
WARNING, LUIZA!
YOU ARE APPLYING DEADLY FORCE TO TARGETS NOT CLASSIFIED AS CRIMINALS.
THEY CAN GET NEW KNEES.

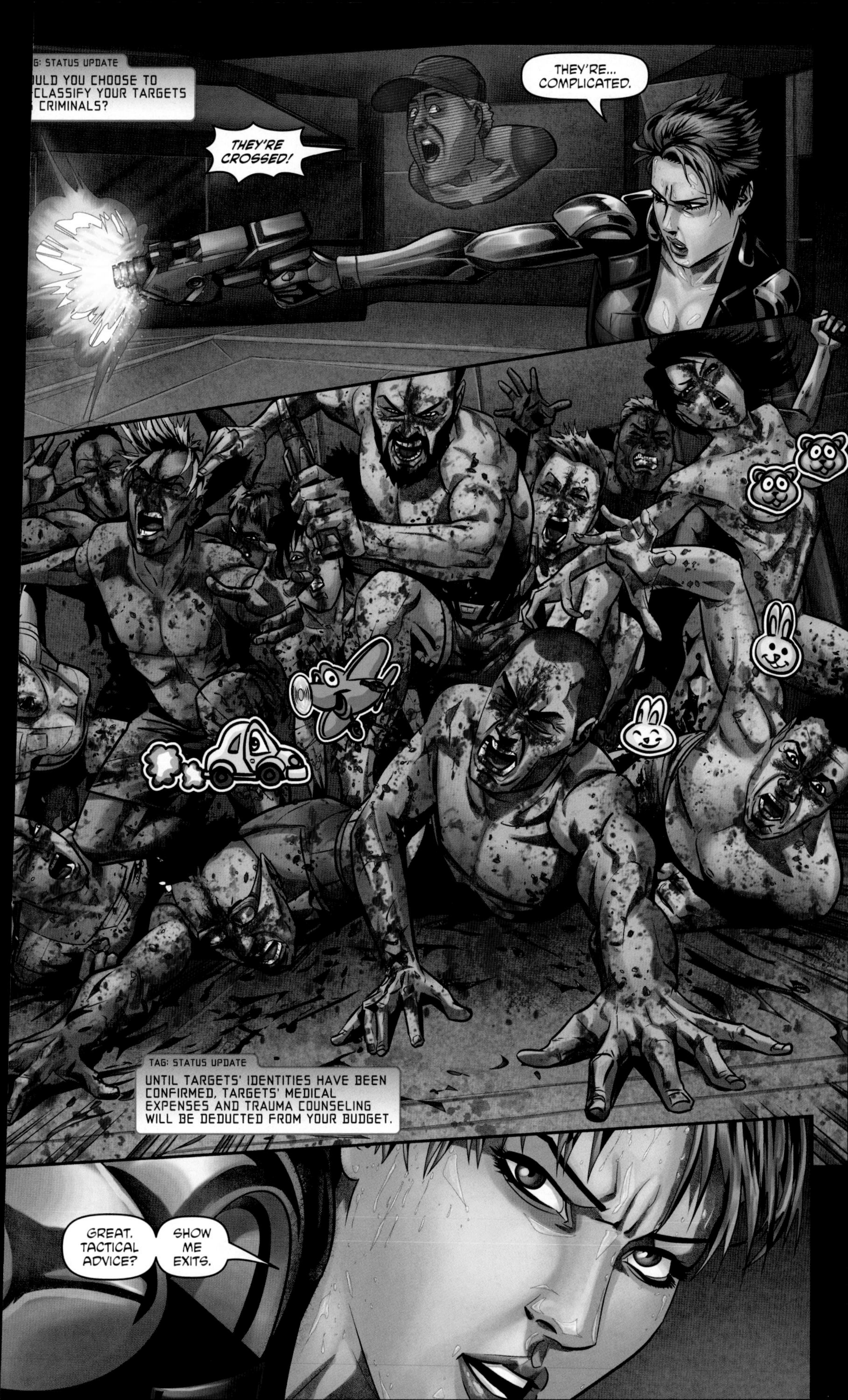
TAG: STATUS UPDATE
ULD YOU CHOOSE TO CLASSIFY YOUR TARGETS CRIMINALS?
THEY'RE... COMPLICATED.
THEY'RE CROSSED!
TAG: STATUS UPDATE
UNTIL TARGETS' IDENTITIES HAVE BEEN CONFIRMED, TARGETS' MEDICAL EXPENSES AND TRAUMA COUNSELING WILL BE DEDUCTED FROM YOUR BUDGET.
GREAT. TACTICAL ADVICE?
SHOW ME EXITS.

TAG: TACTICAL UPDATE
PROCESSING...
TAG: HATCH
LEADS TO CRAWLWAYS.
TAG: TRANSPARENT MATERIAL
CONTROL BAY OBSERVATION PORT. UNCERTAIN RESISTANCE TO FORCE.
TAG: DROP
TOO FAR TO FALL SAFELY.
TAG: TRANSPARENT MATERIAL
HIGH RESISTANCE TO FORCE.
OH WELL.

TAG: STATUS UPDATE
SYNTHETIC MYOFIBER OUTPUT: 172%.
NUCLOSE RESERVOIR AT 37%.
AS IF IT EVER WAS GOING TO BE EASY.

ER... LUIZA.
THEY'VE BITTEN YOU. THAT'S *BAD*.
DON'T DISTRACT ME.
WORKING.

FUCK YOU!
FUCK EVERYONE.
TAG: STATUS UPDATE
NUCLOSE RESERVOIR AT 16%.
WARNING: NUCLOSE RESERVOIR NEAR DEPLETION...

OH CRAP. THAT'S A NASTY BITE YOU'VE GOT THERE.
I'M SO SORRY, LUIZA. YOU WERE A GREAT FRIEND WITH AN AMAZING ASS.
SHUT UP. IT'S JUST A BITE.
YOU'RE *INFECTED*. SALIVA OR OTHER FLUID AND IT'S GOODBYE CIVILIZATION AND HELLO SEXUAL DEVIANCY ON AN AVATAR COMICS SCALE.
DON'T BE PARANOID. THIS ISN'T CROSSED.
IT'S....
LUIZA! SPEAK TO ME!

HUNNNGGGERRRR YOUR CRYSTAL-CLIT!
SOMETHING LIKE THAT, RIGHT?
ARE YOU FUCKING WITH ME?
YES, I'M FUCKING WITH YOU.
THEY'RE NOT CROSSED.
THEY'RE JUST *ACTING* LIKE CROSSED.

YOU'RE BEING PRETTY BLASÉ. IT COULD BE A BIO-PLAGUE, WHICH MEANS IT COULD BE PASSED VIA FLUIDS.
MAYBE IT'S NOT TEN SECONDS TO GOING CROSSED. MAYBE IT'S TEN MINUTES. OR TEN HOURS. YOU CAN'T KNOW.
I'M IMPRESSED, LUCAS.
THAT WAS ALMOST LIKE ACTUAL SCIENTIFIC ADVICE.
MY BIOLOGY WAS ENHANCED TO WORK IN COMBAT ZONES. I'LL KNOW IF I'M INFECTED.
COULD BE A NEW DESIGNER PLAGUE. MAY NOT SHOW. MAY GO FOR THE SYSTEMIC HARDWARE ANALYSIS FIRST, SO YOU WOULDN'T KNOW YOUR VITALS WERE TWITCHING.
IF IT'S NEW, IT COULD BE DESIGNED TO TAKE OUT OLD HARDWARE, WHICH-- I'M SORRY TO BREAK IT TO YOU-- IS YOU.
WHY ARE YOU SO WORRIED? YOU'RE DEAD. WHAT DOES IT MATTER TO YOU?
YOU... YOU COULD EXTRACT ME FROM YOUR HEAD, AND USE ME AS A COLONIC EXPLORATION DEVICE.
YOU'RE CRYSTAL. YOU WOULDN'T BE CONSCIOUS. YOU'D BE A LUMP OF ROCK STUCK UP SOMEONE'S ASS.
I KNOW. IT'S JUST THE *IDEA* OF IT.
DON'T LIKE BUTT STUFF.

I PROMISE
J, LUCAS. NO BUTT
STUFF.
GET
ME
VIKA.
HEY--
LUIZA. ARE YOU
OKAY?
THE
SPIRE IS
DOWN.
COULDN'T GET
A MESSAGE
OUT.
I'M SORRY--
WE DIDN'T KNOW. ARE
YOU OKAY?
I'M FINE.
ANY OTHER
IDEAS?
I GUESS
MAYBE YOU SHOULD
HOLE UP WHILE WE
THINK. GET DOWN TO
SECURITY AND WE'LL
LET YOU IN.
HMM.
NOT
CONVINCED BY
THE PLAN?
MORE
ANNOYED I DON'T HAVE
ONE OF MY OWN.
I'M STARTING TO
FEEL LIKE I'M A RAT RUNNING
A MAZE.

THAT WAS SO COOL.
DO YOU HAVE ENOUGH VOCAL IMPRINTS TO CASSETTEBOY HER?
THINK SO, VIKA.
THIS ISN'T A GOOD IDEA. RIGHT NOW, WE MAY BE ABLE TO LIE OUR WAY OUT OF THIS.
THE SECOND WE GO FURTHER, SHE *HAS* TO DIE.
SHE'S GOING TO DIE, FELIPE. WE'RE GOING TO WATCH.
IT'S GOING TO BE FUCKING AWESOME.
OPEN UP!

SO FUCKING COOL.

'SCUSE ME.
COMING THROUGH.
CROSSED
AND... SPIRE OPERATIONAL AGAIN.

BOOT OUR FAUX COP.
THIS IS LUIZA BORA REPORTING FROM THE BASE. COMMUNICATIONS LIMITED. TECHNICAL ISSUES.
NO IMMEDIATE THREAT. NO SUPPORT REQUIRED. WILL REPORT AS SITUATION SOLIDIFIES.
AFFIRMATIVE, LUIZA. THANKS FOR YOUR KINDLY MAIL.
YOU ARE SO GOOD TO CALL. WE *WERE* WORRYING.
THERE WE GO.
PRIVACY.
GET UP HERE!
YOU DON'T WANT TO MISS IT!

WHERE IS SHE?
SHE'S KICKING OPEN A WAY INTO THE MAIN LEVEL.
JUST TIME FOR MORE POPCORN.
ANY CROSSED NEARBY?
NEXT CROSS-JUNCTION.
HEH. CROSSED JUNCTION!
GIVE HER SOME SPACE. USE AN ULTRASONIC GUIDE...
GOOD... GOOD...

I WAS EXPECTING SOME NORMAL GRUNTS TO COME INVESTIGATE, BUT SHE'S GOT TO BE PACKING MILITARY HARDWARE.
YOU SEE HOW SHE JUMPED UP THE SPIRE? THAT WAS SO FUCKING COOL.
POPCORN!
SALTED?
YUP!
POP CORN
HERE WE GO.

HORSECOCK!
OH NO. A TRAP.
WHAT A SURPRISE.

THAT'S NOT A HORSE COCK.
THANKS FOR THE EXPERT KNOWLEDGE, LUCAS.
COULDN'T DO THIS WITHOUT YOU.
TAG: STATUS UPDATE
NUCLOSE RESERVOIR AT 15%.
TAG: STATUS UPDATE
NUCLOSE: FULL BURN.
I'M SORRY, SIR.

THIS IS NECESSARY.
TAG: STATUS UPDATE
SYNTHETIC MYOFIBER OUTPUT: 897%.

STATUS UPDATE
CLOSE RESERVOIR
LETED.
UH-OH. THAT'S TROUBLE.
IT IS. FIRST THINGS FIRST...
...SEAL THE FUCKING DOOR, LUCAS.
DONE.
WHAT... THE FUCK? WHAT'S HAPPENING? WHERE AM I?
ONE MOMENT, SIR.
I NEED TO TAKE CARE OF SOMETHING BEFORE WE TALK.

SIGNAL LOST
I THINK SHE'S ONTO US.
ROSSE

chapter 10

NAHUEL LOPEZ

TAG: SECURITY CENTRAL, DIO-42 BASE
TO ATTEMPT TO SOLVE THE MYSTERY OF AN APPARENT INFECTION OF THE FICTIONAL CROSSED VIRUS, LUIZA BORA TURNS TO DETECTIVE WORK.
YOU RIPPED OUT MY SPINE!

HE'S TAKING IT WELL.
SHUSH.
I'M SORRY, SIR.
IT WAS NECESSARY.
YOU... YOU MASSACRED EVERYONE?
I'VE KILLED NO ONE. THERE'S BEEN AN INCIDENT BASED UPON THE FICTIONAL CROSSED VIRUS.
PRESUMABLY WHILE UNDER ITS INFLUENCE YOU KILLED EVERYONE IN THE SECURITY STATION.
THE BASE DOES BIOLOGICAL WORK. IT COULD BE A PLAGUE... BUT I'VE BEEN EXPOSED AND DON'T HAVE ANY ILL EFFECTS. THE BASE ALSO DOES WORK IN CRYSTAL, HOWEVER...
THEREFORE WE HAD TO REMOVE YOUR CRYSTAL ARRAY. YOU'VE RETURNED TO NORMAL. THAT SEEMS TO PROVES THE CRYSTAL-ORIGINATED HYPOTHESIS.
YOU RIPPED OUT MY SPINE!

THAT'S WHERE YOUR CRYSTAL DOCKING ARRAY WAS.
YOU'LL BE COMPENSATED, SIR.
OH GOD. OH GOD.
IT'S OKAY, SIR. THIS IS UNDERSTANDABLY A DISTRESSING TIME FOR YOU.
HOWEVER, ONCE YOU'VE COMPOSED YOURSELF, I'D LIKE YOU TO TELL ME EVERYTHING THAT'S HAPPENED IN THE LAST TWENTY-FOUR HOURS...
YOU ARE REALLY BAD WITH THE SOFT STUFF, LUIZA.
I SAID *SHUSH*.

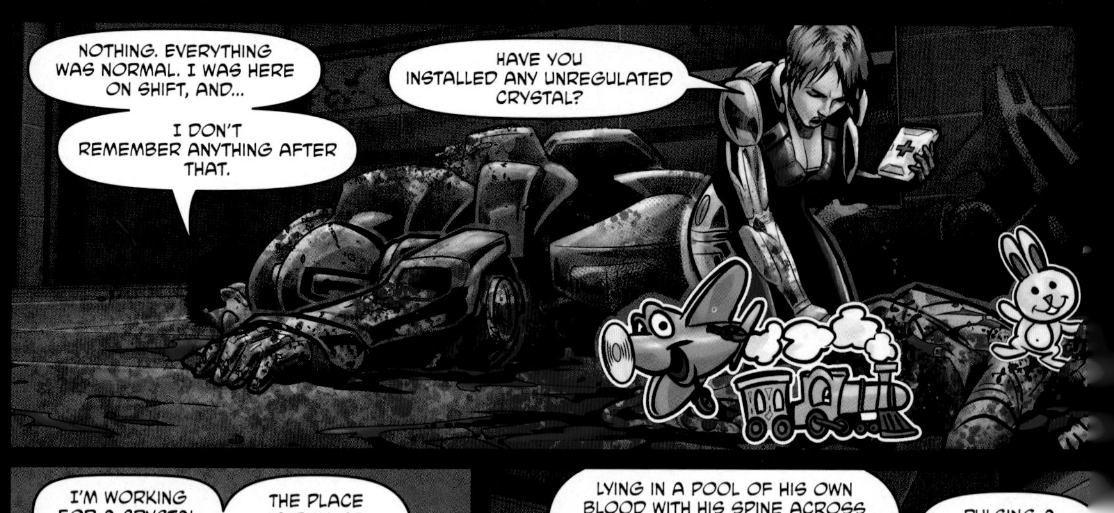
NOTHING. EVERYTHING WAS NORMAL. I WAS HERE ON SHIFT, AND...
HAVE YOU INSTALLED ANY UNREGULATED CRYSTAL?
I DON'T REMEMBER ANYTHING AFTER THAT.

I'M WORKING FOR A CRYSTAL MANUFACTURER.
THE PLACE IS FULL OF UNREGULATED CRYSTAL. IT'S AN OPEN SECRET.
I... IF I TELL YOU ANYTHING, I'M NOT GOING TO END UP LOCKED UP?

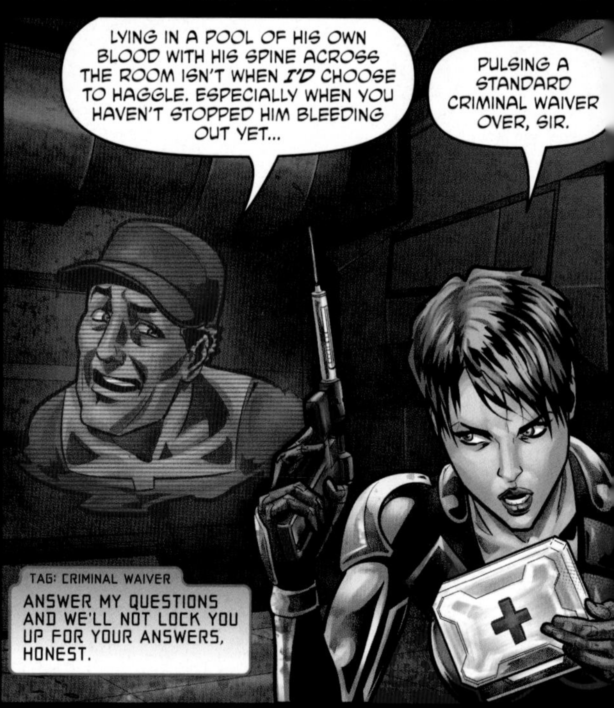
LYING IN A POOL OF HIS OWN BLOOD WITH HIS SPINE ACROSS THE ROOM ISN'T WHEN I'D CHOOSE TO HAGGLE. ESPECIALLY WHEN YOU HAVEN'T STOPPED HIM BLEEDING OUT YET...
PULSING A STANDARD CRIMINAL WAIVER OVER, SIR.
TAG: CRIMINAL WAIVER
ANSWER MY QUESTIONS AND WE'LL NOT LOCK YOU UP FOR YOUR ANSWERS, HONEST.

THE COMPANY GIVES SECURITY ITS COMBAT SKILLS PRE-RELEASE. COULD BE SOMETHING IN THERE?
THIS AFFECTED MORE THAN JUST SECURITY. ANYTHING ELSE?

THIS IS EMBARRASSING...
FELIPE SOLD ME SOMETHING STRAIGHT OFF HIS PRECIPITATOR.

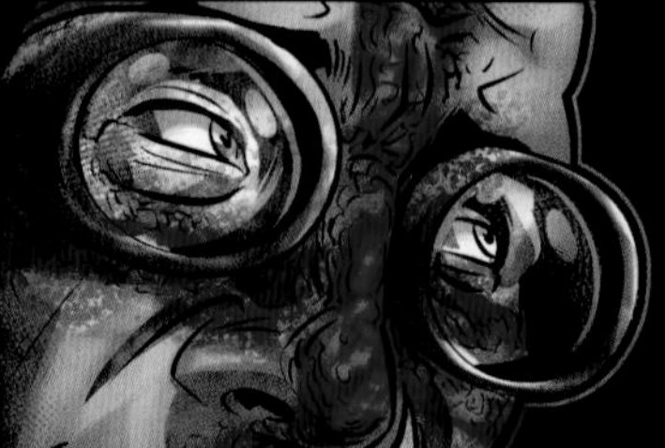
IT WAS AN ORGASM ENHANCER.

OH DO TELL ME MORE!
THAT'S WEIRD. THE BASE IS PRIMARILY MILITARY AND CORPORATE, NOT COMMERCIAL?
IT WAS A PRIVATE PROJECT. MOST OF THE SCIENTISTS WERE ON IT. FOUND OUT MID (ER) COITUS. IT WAS MEMORABLE...
I GOT HOLD OF IT. IT'S GOOD. IT'S *REALLY* GOOD.
IT'S VIKA COX'S PRIVATE PROJECT.
YES. HOW DID YOU KNOW?
OKAY. I'M OUT OF NUCLOSE, BUT THIS IS CENTRAL SECURITY...
THEY'VE GOT COMMUNICATION LOCKED DOWN. WE CAN'T CALL FOR HELP.
WHAT *CAN* WE DO?

VIKA! SHE'S ONTO US! WE'RE FUCKED!
FIRST OF ALL, CALM DOWN, FELIP IT'S NOT THA BAD.
SECOND OF ALL, SHE DOESN'T EVE KNOW WHERE WE ARE.
I KNOW YOU CAN HEAR ME, VIKA. YOU'RE IN THE MAIN SPIRE BUNKER.
I'M COMING FOR YOU.
SHE'S TURNED THE CAMERAS OFF. WE CAN'T TELL WHERE SHE IS OR WHAT SHE'S DOING.
SHE...
FIRE THE ULTRASOUND. GET ALL THE CROSSED BACK UP HERE.
WE NEED A DEFENSIVE LINE.

THIS IS GOING TO BE *TIGHT*.
THEY'VE CALLED THEIR DOGS BACK.
OPEN THE DOOR. SHUT IT AFTER I'M GONE.

I'VE STUCK A CAMERA OF OUR OWN OUTSIDE.
WE'LL SEE IF SHE TRIES TO COME TO OUR DOOR...
THIS IS JUST A HOLDING PATTERN.
WE NEED TO GET AHEAD OF HER.
WE SHOULD GET OUT OF HERE. GO. BLOW THE BASE.
THAT WAS THE NEXT STEP ANYWAY.
NO. SHE COULD BE DOING AN ALIEN AND WAITING AT OUR SHIP.
WE NEED TO *FIND* HER.
SHE'S A PROFESSIONAL. SHE'S GOT MILITARY GRADE CRYSTAL-- AND A DAMN SIGHT BETTER THAN WHAT WE'RE MAKING HERE.
SHE RIPPED OUT OUR ONE-TON HEAD OF SECURITY'S SPINE!
I KNOW. IT WAS AWESOME. BUT SHE'S JUST A PROFESSIONAL.
I'M A *GENIUS*.
I'M A GENIUS TOO.
BUT *I'M* A GENIUS WITH THE BEST IDEA SINCE FRIDAY THE 13TH PART LXXIV: JASON VS. MEGATRON VS MY PRODIGIOUSLY ENDOWED PONY.

THIS MAKES ME NERVOUS.
OF COURSE YOU ARE. WHAT'S THE POINT OF A GOOD HORROR MOVIE IF YOU DON'T GET NERVOUS?
I'M NOT NERVOUS. I'M PETRIFIED.
EVEN BETTER! I AM TOO.
BULLSHIT. OU'RE NOT NERVOUS, VIKA.
WELL, REAL GOREFIENDS LIKE ME ALWAYS WANT THE BIGGER KICK. I'M LOOKING FOR THE ULTIMATE...
...DONE.
PERFECT.

NOW... WHERE WOULD SHE BE?
TAG: NUCLOSE VAULT
WHERE THEY KEEP THE NUCLOSE, OBV.

SURE YOU *NEED* THE NUCLOSE?
YOU PUNCHED THE SHIT OUT OF HIM.
WAIT... TROUBLE. THEY'RE FIRING AN ULTRASOUND WHISTLE FROM *HERE*. THEY'LL BE COMING SOON...
I'D HURRY. THAT'S WHAT I'D DO.
TAG: NUCLOSE LOCK
NUCLOSE LOCK ENGAGED.
ER... LUIZA.
BEHIND YOU.

EXITS?
TAG: STATUS UPDATE
ER.... THE DOOR YOU CAME IN?

GREAT.
NOW THIS IS WHAT WE'VE BEEN WAITING TO SEE.
WE KNOW WHERE SHE IS. SO WE KNOW WHERE SHE *ISN'T*.
WE SHOULD MOVE WHILE WE'VE GOT THE CHANCE.
I WANT TO WATCH IT LIVE!
THERE'S ALWAYS RERUNS.
I GUESS I WOULDN'T WANT TO MISS THE THIRD ACT CLIMAX. HEY, BASE?
ACTIVATE PROCEDURE: ONLY WAY TO BE SURE.
ACTIVATED.
WE ARE LEAVING!

TAG: STATUS UPDATE
5 MINUTES LATER.
OKAY, PREP THIS SUCKER...
HELLO.
I AM OFFICER LUIZA BORA.
YOU ARE UNDER ARREST.

RAISE YOUR HANDS AND DROP TO YOUR KNEES. QUICKLY.
OR DON'T, AND SEE WHAT HAPPENS.
GROSSED
HOW... HOW ARE YOU HERE?
THE CAMERAS AREN'T DEACTIVATED. YOU JUST DIDN'T HAVE ACCESS TO THEM.
DOOKUS COULD SEE WHICH WAY YOU WENT, AND LED ME HERE.
SO YOU FINALLY LET RIP WITH A TANK FULL OF NUCLOSE?
(WHICH IS PRETTY FUCKING KICK-ASS, I HAVE TO SAY.)
YOUR PRINCIPLES CRUMBLE WHEN YOU'RE AGAINST THE WALL, MISS HERO?
I HAVEN'T KILLED ANYONE, VIKA.

SAY 'THEY'LL LIVE'. SAY 'THEY'LL LIVE'. TRUST ME!
THEY'LL LIVE.
OH, TO THE CONTRARY. THE BASE IS SET TO DESTRUCT.
THE WHOLE PLACE GOES UP IN... ONE MINUTE.

AND YOU WITH IT.
I COULD LEAVE YOU HERE AND NO ONE WOULD KNOW.
MAYBE THAT'LL GIVE YOU THE MOTIVATION TO TURN IT OFF...
PLEASE. WE CAN'T DEACTIVATE. IT'S TOO LATE.
HMM. THERE'S A TERMINAL ASCADE GOING ON. AS FAR AS MY TECHNICAL SKILLS CAN TELL, HE'S RIGHT. WE STAY HERE, WE'RE DUST.
OF COURSE, I KNOW FUCK ALL, SO IT'S YOUR CALL. YOU'RE THE ONE WHO'S ALIVE AND EVERYTHING.
DON'T BEG, FELIPE. SHE'S NOT GOING TO LEAVE US HERE.
ISN'T THAT RIGHT, *HERO?*
YOU HAVE NO IDEA WHO I AM.
GET ABOARD THE SHIP.

LUIZA TO SECURITY CENTRAL...
ARE YOU THERE?
WHAT'S UP?
I WAS THINKING...
DO YOU HAVE ANY LOVED ONES?
ANYONE YOU'D LIKE T GET A MESSA TO? IF THIS GO WRONG?
NO ONE WHO DOESN'T KNOW I LOVE THEM.
IS SOMETHING WRONG?
NO, EVERYTHING'S-- ER-- FINE.
BACK-- ERM-- SHORTLY.

WHOA.
A TROJAN PERSONALITY BURIED IN BLACK CRYSTAL, DISTRIBUTED FOR FREE, THEN ACTIVATED.
WHY DID YOU DO IT?
WE WANTED TO HAVE A LITTLE FUN.
I WON'T TALK UNTIL WE GET A LAWYER CRYSTAL.
BUT REALLY? JUST BETWEEN ME AND YOU, LUIZA.
ROSS
TAG: CITADEL 57
CURRENT HOME TO THE NOMADIC BELT WORKERS AND SUPPORT, CONSISTING OF 95% OF THE PRESENT POPULATION OF MERCURY. ESTIMATED TO BE UPWARDS OF 3 MILLION PEOPLE.

TAG: STATUS UPDATE
3 MILLION AND FALLING.

A LITTLE FUN TO BEGIN WITH... THEN A LOT OF FUN TO FINISH.

chapter 11
NAHUEL LÓPEZ 2016

: CITADEL 57
RRENT OPERATIVE PLUG
SE. CURRENTLY INVOLVED
A QUASI-CROSSED
URSION.
GRAPEVINE! FILL ME IN!
WHAT'S HAPPENED WHILE I WAS AWAY?
GOOD NEWS, LUIZA!
THERE ARE *MANY* RELEVANT TASKS BASED UPON YOUR SKILL-SET, EXPERIENCE, PRICE AND--

YAY! THAT'S ONE OF THEM!
AND THAT'S ANOTHER!
AND THAT'S A THIRD!
PAYMENT IS PROCESS--

OH, BELAY THAT.
TAG: STATUS UPDATE
SYNTHETIC MYOFIBER OUTPUT: 188%.

AND *THAT'S* A THIRD!

WELL DONE, CA. THE PROCEEDS E BEEN DEPOSITED D YOUR ACCOUNT!
TASKS CONTINUE. FOR EXAMPLE, A CROSSED COMING AT YOU, A CROSSED COMING AT YOU, A CROSSED COMING AT YOU, A CROSSED--
FORGET IT. BACK ABOARD THE SHIP, GENIUS PSYCHOS.
THE LEVEL OF CRISIS HAS OVERWHELMED GRAPEVINE.
NO IT HASN'T. IT'S JUST THAT SHE HAS TOO MUCH INFORMATION TO GIVE YOU.
SHE COULD UPLOAD THINGS DIRECTLY TO YOUR READ/WRITE CRYSTALS, BUT THAT BREAKS EVERY PRIVACY LAW WE HAVE.
INSTEAD, SHE HAS TO BABBLE UNTIL YOU GIVE HER PERMISSION.
WHO DIED AND MADE YOU TECH GOD?
WELL, *I* DIED AND IT MADE ME SLIGHTLY MORE COMPETENT, AS NOW I GET ACCESS TO SOME DATABASE MEMORY BANKS INSTEAD OF TRYING TO MEMORISE WHAT YOUR ASS LOOKS LIKE FOR MY SPANK BANK.
UGH.
SO... SOMETHING RUNNING ON YOUR UI JUST MADE YOU SHIVER IN A WAY THAT NOTHING ELSE HAS.
WHAT KIND OF MONSTER HAVE YOU GOT UP THERE?
I DON'T SHARE *MY* PERSONAL HORRORS.
WITH LUCK, YOU'LL NEVER KNOW.

LUCAS-- GET JEANETTE Y OR WHOEVER'S ALIVE IN HOTSIDE CENTRAL.
AFFIRMATIVE.
I DON'T HAVE TIME FOR THIS.
WE'RE IN A CRITICAL SITUATION HERE. I--
I'VE GOT THE CULPRITS.
THEY'VE BEEN MAKING BLACK MARKET CRYSTAL WITH SOMETHING BURIED IN IT THAT TURNS PEOPLE INTO CROSSED. ALMOST THE WHOLE BASE WAS INFECTED BY THE TIME I GOT THERE. THEY SET IT TO DETONATE.
SO THE MESSAGE THAT YOU WERE FINE... WAS FAKED. I UNDERSTAND. GOOD WORK.
SEND ME WHAT YOU'VE GOT.
I'LL HAVE LUCAS UPLOAD ALL THE DATA I HAVE FROM THERE.
DONE! LOOK AT ME, BEING ALL EFFICIENT!
HAVE YOU INTERROGATED THEM?
I DON'T HAVE THE HARDWARE. OR THE CLEARANCE.
I'LL GET GRAPEVINE TO SET A MISSION.
THERE'LL BE AN AGENT WITH YOU SHORTLY.

LAST CHANCE TO TALK BEFORE THE HEAVY DUTY HARDWARE ARRIVES. WHAT'S GOING ON HERE?
WE'LL COOPERATE!
WIMP.
WE'RE THE PEOPLE BEHIND THE UPSURGE OF BLACK MARKET CRYSTAL.
IT'S ALL BEEN LEAKED ONTO THE MARKET BY US. HIGH-END COMBAT TECH. LOW-END SEXUAL STIMULANTS...
ALL OF IT HAS MY CROSSED ROUTINE.
WHEN THE CONTROLLING SIGNAL WAS STOPPED, THE ROUTINE ACTIVATED.
WE STOPPED IT WHEN WE BLEW UP OUR BASE. NOW, IT'S C-DAY FOR EVERYONE.
HOW DO YOU DEACTIVATE THE ROUTINE?
YOU CAN'T.
I DON'T BELIEVE YOU, WHICH MEANS YOU'RE GOING TO HAVE TO FACE THE INQUISITION.
HOPE YOU'RE READY FOR THAT.
AGENT'S OUTSIDE. SAYS THE AREA HAS BEEN PACIFIED.
OPENING!

N'GAI!
I'M FINE.
IT'S ONLY HALF MY BODY.
MOTHER NATURE SAW FIT TO GIFT ME WITH ANOTHER 50%.
THAT LINE RINGS A BELL.
N'GAI... ARE YOU RUNNING THE CHEAP ACTION MOVIE DIALOGUE PLUG-IN?
MAYBE.
I INCAPACITATED EVERYONE, SO WE'VE GOT A WINDOW, BUT IT'S SMALL.
GOOD LUCK.
NO! NOT AN INTERROGATION!
FUCK YOU, FELIPE. WE CAN TAKE IT.

CAN THEY TURN OFF THE QUANTUM CRYSTAL?
NO :(
FUCK IT. ALL FOR NOTHING.
JEANETTE Y. THERE'S NO SIMPLE TURN OFF, UNLESS HE'S GOT A WAY TO CIRCUMVENT THE LIE DETECTOR.
IF HE HAS, WE'LL NEED THE HIGH TECH HERE. IF HE HASN'T, WE'LL NEED MORE TIME TO TRY AND WORK OUT WHAT TO DO.
EITHER WAY, WE NEED TO INTERROGATE THEM PROPERLY. HOTSIDE CENTRAL IS CHAOS. YOU WON'T GET TWO CIVILIANS ALL THE WAY HERE.
USE YOUR KIMMER, GET TO E ELEVATOR, AND SCEND TO ORBIT. ERE'S TROUBLE UP THERE, BUT IT'S RELATIVELY QUIET.
GOOD LUCK, LUIZA.
YOU COULD ALWAYS FLOOD THE WHOLE CITADEL-PLUG WITH SOME TOP LEVEL NERVE TOXINS...
IMAGINE, EVERYONE OUT THERE JUST REDUCED TO BAGS OF TWITCHING MUSCLE. FUCKING AWESOME.
IT'D BE A SHAME IF VIKA JUST FELL OUT OF AN AIRLOCK...
WE DO HAVE A SPARE INFORMANT...
AS MUCH AS IT HURTS TO ADMIT IT, I GET THE AWFUL FEELING VIKA IS THE BRAINS.
WE NEED HIM.

COMING?
NO. I'VE GOT GRAPEVINE TO SEND A PICK-UP MISSION TO ME. I WON'T LAST INTO ORBIT, AND IT'S GOING TO BE HARD ENOUGH FOR YOU TO CARRY TWO PEOPLE, LET ALONE A THIRD.
THANKS. I... I GUESS I'VE GOT TO GET ON WITH THIS CASE.
SEE. THE SYSTEM WORKS.
GOOD LUCK, LUIZA.
GGRRRR.
GREAT.
LOWER YOUR WEAPONS.
YOU ARE UNDER ARREST!

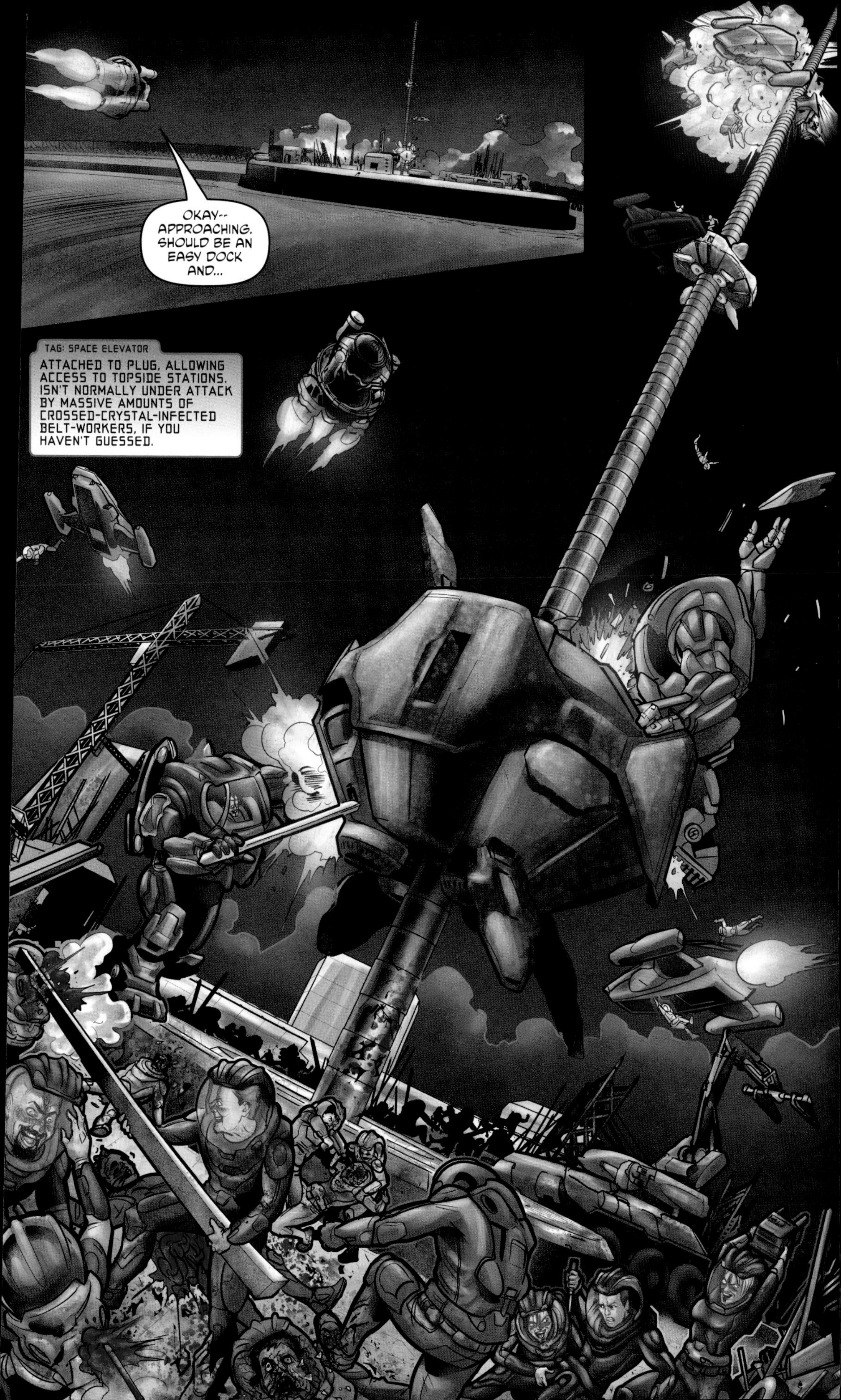
OKAY--
APPROACHING.
SHOULD BE AN
EASY DOCK
AND...
TAG: SPACE ELEVATOR
ATTACHED TO PLUG, ALLOWING ACCESS TO TOPSIDE STATIONS. ISN'T NORMALLY UNDER ATTACK BY MASSIVE AMOUNTS OF CROSSED-CRYSTAL-INFECTED BELT-WORKERS, IF YOU HAVEN'T GUESSED.

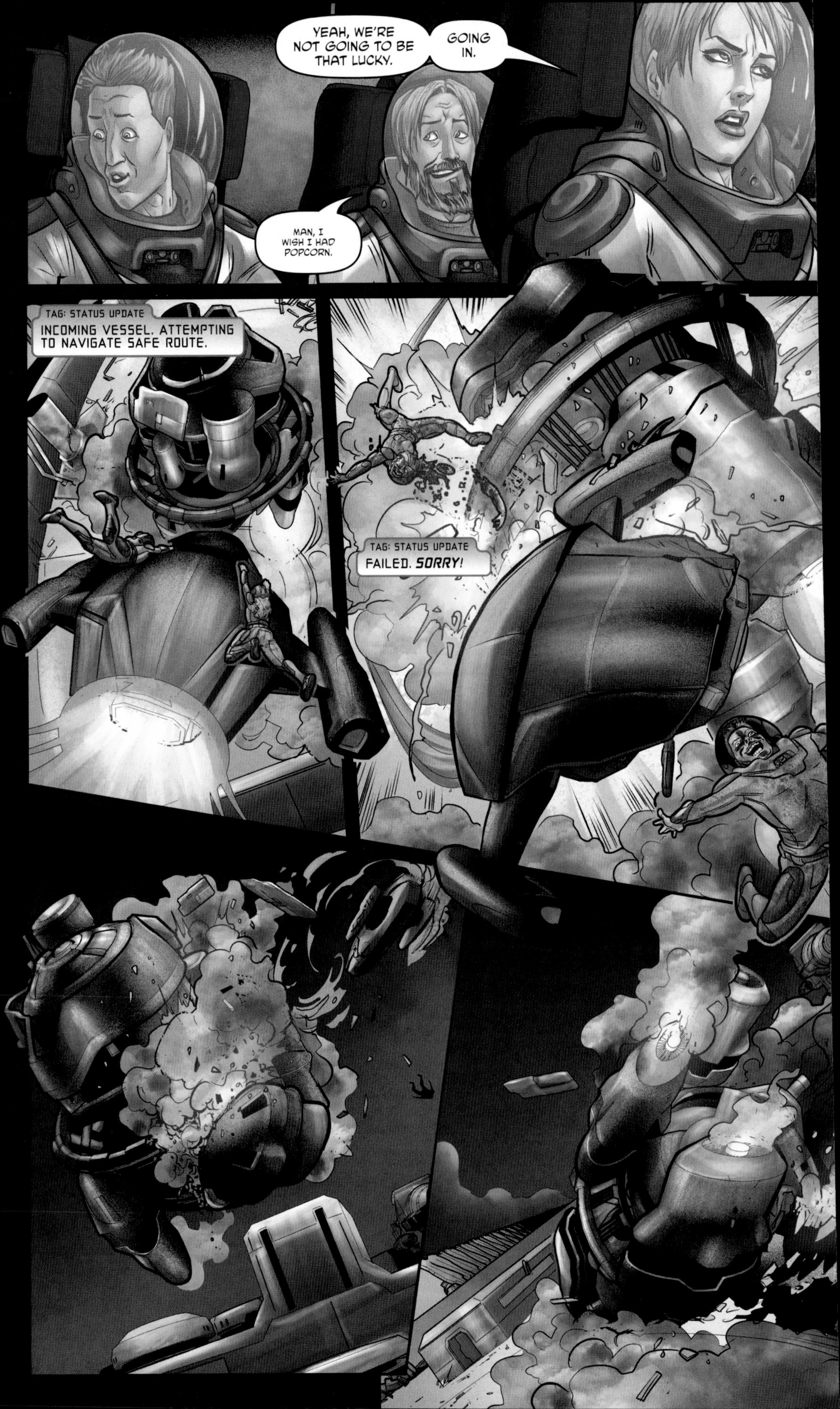
YEAH, WE'RE NOT GOING TO BE THAT LUCKY.
GOING IN.
MAN, I WISH I HAD POPCORN.
TAG: STATUS UPDATE
INCOMING VESSEL. ATTEMPTING TO NAVIGATE SAFE ROUTE.
TAG: STATUS UPDATE
FAILED. SORRY!

DON'T RUN! YOU'LL DIE OUT THERE!
HAH! SHOWS WHAT YOU KNOW!
WHAT THE FUCK...
SEAL THE DOOR!

OH NO! NOW YOU CAN'T GET TO THE SPACE ELEVATOR!
SHE'S TRAPPED! WHAT'S THE LAST HOPE FOR HUMANITY GOING TO DOOOOOOO-OOO?
LUCAS? PATCH ME UP TO TOPSIDE SECURITY.
GET ME SIMON HARKING.
I'LL GET LUIZA'S BOYFRIENNNNND.
PLEASE, LUCAS. DON'T.

LUIZA. AREN'T
MEANT TO BE BRINGING
E FUCKWITS BEHIND ALL
THIS UP HERE?
WE CAN'T MAKE IT TO THE ELEVATOR.
CAN YOU DROP US A SHIP TO THESE COORDINATES?
SURE.
NOW... I HATE TO SAY THIS, BUT ARE WE TALKING AGAIN? DO WE ONLY FLIRT WHEN IT'S THE END OF THE WORLD?
I HAVEN'T
OT TIME FOR
THIS.
I DON'T KNOW WHAT IT'S LIKE UP THERE, BUT IT'S A FUCKING MESS DOWN HERE.
IT'S NOT GREAT HERE EITHER. THE TECHS ARE MOST LIKELY TO HAVE INFECTED CRYSTAL. VERY LITTLE IN OUR SECURITY. THE NEW ARRIVALS OBVIOUSLY DON'T HAVE ANY.
IT'S BAD, BUT IT'S AS SAFE AS IT GETS.
SHIP DROPPING. WITH YOU IN FIVE.
SEE YOU SHORT--
LUCAS! WHAT HAVE YOU DONE!
IT'S NOT ME! SIGNAL DROPPED. DISRUPTION IN THE SIGNAL LINK UP THE ELEVATOR.
HEY, I THINK I CAN GUESS THE PROBLEM...

THIS SORT OF THING HAPPENS A OT WHEN WE HANG OUT, LUIZA.
DO YOU THINK THE UNIVERSE MAY BE TRYING TO GIVE US A SIGN?
LET'S HOPE HE DROPPED THE SHIP. IT'S OUR ONLY WAY OUT OF HERE.
WELL, YOU'RE NOT GOING TO BE ABLE TO TAKE ME ANY FURTHER WITHOUT GETTING YOURSELF KILLED.
YOU SEEM AWFULLY CALM ABOUT DYING. ARE YOU REALLY THAT BLANK?

NO, I'M NOT GOING TO DIE, AT LEAST NOT FROM *MY* GUYS.
ONLY GETS BAD FOR ME IF YOU GET THIS ALL UNDER CONTROL... THEN I'M IN A CELL, BEING INTERVIEWED BY A BUNCH OF PSYCHOLOGISTS LOOKING TO MAKE THEIR NAME.
AFTER LEAVING MERCURY AS A MURDERZONE? I'M AN INTERESTING SERIAL KILLER.
HOW'RE YOU GOING TO DO THAT WHEN YOU'RE TORN APART BY YOUR OWN INVENTIONS?
PLEASE. FELIPE AND ME AREN'T TARGETS. THAT'S THE OTHER PART OF THE HARD-CODING.
I COULD WALK THROUGH HERE TAKING PHOTOS, SHOOTING THEM THROUGH THE HEAD AND BEATING OFF INTO THE FLESH WOUNDS. THEY WON'T CARE.
I GET TO WATCH. THIS IS AL FOR ME.
OKAY. I GET IT.
TELL ME WHY.
WHY SHOULD I DO A THING LIKE THAT?
IF I'VE LEARNED ANYTHING ABOUT YOU, VIKA, IT'S THAT YOU LIKE TO GLOAT.
AND THIS MAY BE THE LAST CHANCE YOU'RE GOING TO GET.
WE WERE CHEATED.

DO YOU KNOW HOW BAD THINGS LOOKED IN THE 21ST CENTURY?
IT WAS ALL GOING TO COME CRUMBLING DOWN AND WE'D GET TO BE MEN IN THE RUINS. THERE WAS NO FUTURE AND IT WAS GOING TO BE AMAZING.
IT *HAUNTED* ALL THOSE STORIES. WE KNEW WE WERE SO FUCKING DOOMED, AND ALL THOSE WRITERS REVELED IN IT. IT WAS FREEING. NO SOCIETY, NO RULES, NO HUMANITY.
AND THEN WE FOUND A WAY INTO *THIS* FUTURE.
AND IT'S ALL SO... MESSY. SO SMALL. SO UNGLAMOROUS. NO ROOM FOR HEROES STANDING IN THE ASHES.
I WANTED FOR ONCE IN MY LIFE TO SEE THE FUTURE WE WERE PROMISED.
I WANTED IT FOR REAL.
AND YOU HAVE TO ADMIT, IT'S PRETTY AWESOME.
SO YOU'RE SAYING THIS IS JUST YOUR FANFIC?
I OBJECT.
FANFIC IS FOR LITTLE GIRLS.
THIS IS FOR GROWN-UPS.
THANKS, VIKA.
IT'S GOOD TO KNOW.

GO FOR IT. IT'D BE A NICE ENDING.
EVIL GENIUS FINALLY BREAKS WILL OF NOBLE COP.
YOU THINK YOU'RE SO COOL.
EMOTION DAMPENERS TAKE THE EDGE OFF THE FEAR.
BUT REALLY? I GOT WHAT I WANTED. I'VE ALREADY WON. THIS IS ALL JUST MY VICTORY LAP.
GOT TO BE HONEST, IF YOU WANT TO END HIM, I DON'T BLAME YOU.
BUT BE QUICK...
"...YOUR NOT-BOYFRIEND'S SHUTTLE IS INCOMING."
YOU'LL GET WHAT YOU DESERVE, VIKA.

TAG: STATUS UPDATE
SYNTHETIC MYOFIBER OUTPUT: 162%.
IT ALL LOOKS SO PEACEFUL FROM UP HERE...

ACTUALLY, NO, IT DOESN'T. IT LOOKS LIKE THE END OF THE FUCKING WORLD.
WHAT WAS I THINKING?

chapter 12

NAHUEL LOPEZ

POP
OSSED
POP

I DO LOVE A HAPPY ENDING...

...OF ALL LIFE ON MERCURY.

COMING IN TO DOCK, HARKING...
TAG: TOPSIDE CENTRAL
NORMALLY CONNECTED TO PLANET WITH A SPACE ELEVATOR. PRESENTLY NOT, AS THE SPACE ELEVATOR HAS EJECTED AND IS NOW CRASHING ACROSS THE SURFACE OF MERCURY.
LUIZA. DON'T CALL ME HARKING.
CALL ME SIMON.
OOOOOHHH! CALL ME SIIIMMMMON.
THE DOCKS SHOULD BE CLEAR.
I'LL MEET YOU THERE.

CUNTZZZ!
CUNTZZZ!
TAG: COMBAT MODS
ACTIVE.
KLLK!
KLLK!

I'M SORRY. I.T. SAID THE DOCK WAS CLEAR.
FORGET IT. THE DOCK IS CLEAR NOW.
DO YOU HAVE A GRAPEVINE CORE ABOARD?
OF COURSE, I--
JUST GET ME THERE.
I KNOW HOW TO STOP THIS.

HEY, FELIPE!
VIKA!
YOU GOT AWAY FROM THE COP! NICELY PLAYED.
POPCORN?
POP CORN
THANKS, MAN.
OSS
ETTING... PRETTY HAIRY.
WHAT'S THE NEXT MOVE?
POP CORN
EVERYONE DIES AND IT ALL CALMS DOWN. EVENTUALLY I GET ARRESTED AND HAVE A BIG TRIAL WHERE I GET TO DO MY SPEECHES.
I HAVE LOTS OF SPEECHES. THEY ARE ALL VERY COOL.
PROBLEM IS, I WAS PRETTY SURE YOU'D HAVE DIED BY NOW, BEING MY SIDEKICK AND ALL.
OSS
POP CORN

AND I REALLY WANT TO BE THE SOLE GENIUS.
WE DON'T WANT TO OVER-COMPLICATE THE NARRATIVE.
PEOPLE JUST WOULDN'T GET IT.
POP CORN
POP CORN

HEY, GRAPEVINE CORE!
I NEED YOU TO FORCE-UPLOAD A PROGRAM TO ANYONE WITH A READ/WRITE CRYSTAL.
I'M SORRY, LUIZA. THIS IS IN CONTRAVENTION OF THE UZ ACT OF THE EARLY 21ST CENTURY.
THIS BREAKS MANY KEY CIVIC STATUTES...
WE'RE IN A STATE OF MARTIAL DISORDER.
CIVIC STATUTES CAN BE SUSPENDED ACCORDING TO HEAT AUTHORITY...
HMM. WE'VE REESTABLISHED A LINK WITH PLANETSIDE. LET ME CHECK IN WITH JEANETTE Y FOR CLEARANCE.
JEANETTE?

AARRGHH!
TAG: HOTSIDE CENTRAL
LINES ARE BUSY AT THE MOMENT. YOU HAVE BEEN PLACED IN A QUEUE.
HMM. JEANETTE Y ISN'T ANSWERING.
I'M THE RANKING HEAT OFFICER PRESENT.
I HAVE CLEARANCE.
WHAT DO YOU WANT?
CERTAINLY, LUIZA. IF YOU THINK IT'S BEST...

UPLOAD MY CENSORSHIP APP. 'ROSE TINTERS.' IT'S FREE.
BEFORE DOING SO, TURN ON A CENSOR PROGRAM AND SET IT TO...
"IF A HUMAN DOES NOT EQUAL VIKA COX, THEN DISPLAY THEM AS VIKA COX."
VERY WELL.
WHAT IF IT ALREADY EQUALS VIKA?
CHRIST, I DON'T CARE. MAKE HIM A FLUFFY BUNNY!
JUST DO IT! PEOPLE ARE DYING!
AFFIRMATIVE, LUIZA.
PROGRAM UPLOADING NOW...

TAG: STATUS UPDATE
UPLOAD DETECTED.
TAG: STATUS UPDATE
'ROSE TINTERS' INSTALLED!
TAG: STATUS UPDATE
CRYSTAL ACTIVATED!
LUIZA... I'M GETTING REPORTS OF VIOLENCE CEASING.
QUASI-CROSSED ARE JUST STANDING THERE...
VIKA SET THEM NOT TO ATTACK ANYONE WHO LOOKS LIKE HIM.
98% OF THE POPULATION HAVE READ/WRITE CRYSTAL OF SOME SORT. WE CAN HANDLE 2%.
I DO BELIEVE WE'VE SAVED THE FUCKING DAY!

BUNNNNEEEEZZZ.
HUH?

TAG: STATUS UPDATE
FOUR HOURS LATER.
THIS IS *YOUR* MESS, LUIZA.

T'S ACTUALLY VIKA'S SS. AS IN, THIS MESS IS TERALLY VIKA'S BODY PARTS.
SHE'S TALKING FIGURATIVELY...
I KNOW. IT WAS A VIKA-STYLE JOKE.
I'M PAYING RESPECTS, IN MY OWN WAY.
SHUSH.
WHILE YOU FINDING A SOLUTION IS VIOUSLY COMMENDABLE, ESTIONS WILL BE ASKED BOUT WHAT HAPPENED TO VIKA...
YOUR ACTIONS DIRECTLY LEAD TO HIS DEATH.
IT WAS A DISASTER STATE. EVERY SECOND, PEOPLE WERE DYING. I HAD TO ACT SWIFTLY. I DIDN'T THINK IT THROUGH.
I TAKE FULL RESPONSIBILITY.
IT'S AN IRONIC ENDING...
FROM WHAT I SAW IN THE PERPETRATOR'S PROFILE, IT'S THE WAY HE'D HAVE WANTED TO GO...
YOU ARE TO RECEIVE A COMMENDATION IN YOUR FILE FOR QUICK THINKING...

...HOWEVER, YOU ARE NOW SUBJECT TO AN INVESTIGATION.
DATA PRIVACY LOBBYISTS ARE TOUCHY AND YOU BREACHED THE PRIVACY OF 98% OF MERCURY'S CITIZENS.
QUESTIONS HAVE BEEN RAISED ON YOUR SUITABILITY FOR GENERAL POLICING DUE TO YOUR LACK OF INTEREST IN THE RULE OF CIVILIZED LAW.
UNTIL FURTHER NOTICE, YOU'LL BE ONLY OFFERED THE MOST EXTREME CASES WHERE OPERATION OUTSIDE SUCH BOUNDARIES IS ACCEPTABLE.
SO I ONLY GET TO DEAL WITH *THIS* LEVEL OF STUFF?
BASICALLY, YES.
ON THE BRIGHT SIDE, ROSE TINTERS INC HAVE SENT A BASKET OF MUFFINS OVER TO THANK YOU...
...WHICH WILL BE CONFISCATED AND DESTROYED IN ACCORDANCE WITH OUR GUIDELINES AGAINST GIFTS AND/OR BRIBES.

CAN ROSE TINTERS INC AT LEAST GIVE ME THE AD-FREE VERSION OF THE APP?
I'LL CHECK...
THEY SAY NO.
HEY, LUIZA. GOOD WORKING TOGETHER. WHAT ARE YOU DOING LATER?
SORRY, SIMON. NO. REALLY, NO. I THINK I MAY BE A LESBIAN AND/OR DEAD.
SO...
YOU'RE A LESBIAN? A ZOMBIE LESBIAN?
CAN I WATCH?
PLEASE!!!!

I NEED AN AB-1, ANI.
AND... DO YOU HAVE A HAMMER?
DON'T THINK SO.
JUST THE DRINK THEN.
GRAPEVINE?
YES, LUIZA. ARE YOU SMARTING OVER THE SITUATION? I KNOW IT'S UNFORTUNATE, BUT--
NO, JUST HAVING A DRINK.
YOUR DRINKING MAY BE BECOMING A PROBLEM. THIS WILL ADVERSELY AFFECT FUTURE--
THANKS, GRAPEVINE. BUT I WANT TO POST A MISSION!
I NEED A HAMMER. AS SOON AS POSSIBLE.
THIS IS A PRIORITY CLASS-- MISSION.
A DAY'S WAGE FOR A HAMMER?
YOU MUST REALLY WANT A HAMMER.
THAT I DO.

LOOK ON THE BRIGHT SIDE, LUIZA. YOU'RE ALIVE.
AND IT WAS AN ADVENTURE, WASN'T IT?
I MEAN, YOU HAD THE CENSORS RUNNING BUT YOU MISSED SOME REALLY AWESOME STUFF. THERE WAS ONE BIT WHERE THIS GIRL'S TITS HAD--
HAMMER FOR LUIZA BORA!
OVER HERE!
OUTBOARD, EJECT LUCAS' CRYSTAL.
TAG: STATUS UPDATE
CERTAINLY, LUIZA.
WAIT, WHAT ARE YOU--

DO YOU HAVE A DUSTPAN AND BRUSH?
THAT, I CAN HELP WITH.

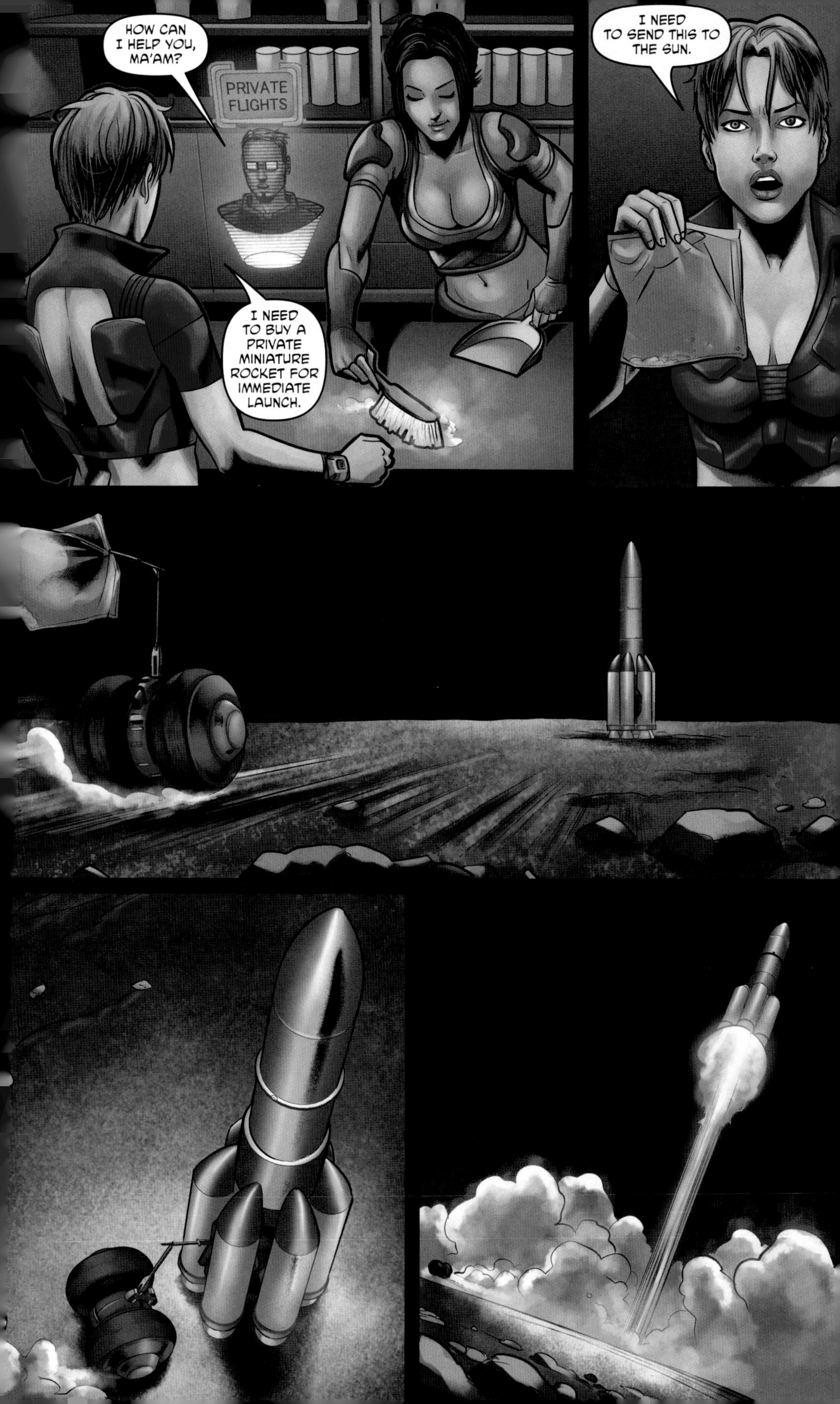
HOW CAN I HELP YOU, MA'AM?
PRIVATE FLIGHTS
I NEED TO BUY A PRIVATE MINIATURE ROCKET FOR IMMEDIATE LAUNCH.
I NEED TO SEND THIS TO THE SUN.

I'M GOING
TO COUNT THIS AS
A WIN.